A Worldly Country

ALSO BY JOHN ASHBERY

A Worldly Country

NEW POEMS

JOHN ASHBERY

An Imprint of HarperCollins*Publishers*

FIRST ECCO PAPERBACK PUBLISHED 2008.

Designed by Cassandra J. Pappas

Library of Congress Cataloging-in-Publication Data is available upon request.

ISBN: 978-0-06-117384-4 (pbk.)

08 09 10 11 12 ID/RRD 10 9 8 7 6 5 4 3 2 1

in memory of Barbara Epstein

ACKNOWLEDGMENTS

The author gratefully acknowledges the following publications in which poems in *A Worldly Country* first appeared, sometimes in slightly different form: *Aphros, Bard Papers, Boston Review, Canary, Chicago Review, Cimarron, Conduit, Conjunctions, Crazyhorse, Crowd, Denver Quarterly, Gingko Tree Review, Interim, Jubilat, LIT, The London Review of Books, Lungfull, McSweeney's, New Review of Literature, The New York Review of Books, The New Yorker, No, The Paris Review, PN Review, Raritan,* and *The Times Literary Supplement.*

"Mottled Tuesday" was first published as a broadside by the Dia Art Foundation on the occasion of John Ashbery's reading at Dia:Beacon on 11 June 2006.

"Feverfew" was first published in *Something Understood: Essays on Poetry and Poems for Helen Vendler.*

CONTENTS

A Worldly Country

A Worldly Country

Not the smoothness, not the insane clocks on the square,
the scent of manure in the municipal parterre,
not the fabrics, the sullen mockery of Tweety Bird,
not the fresh troops that needed freshening up. If it occurred
in real time, it was OK, and if it was time in a novel
that was OK too. From palace and hovel
the great parade flooded avenue and byway
and turnip fields became just another highway.
Leftover bonbons were thrown to the chickens
and geese, who squawked like the very dickens.
There was no peace in the bathroom, none in the china closet
or the banks, where no one came to make a deposit.
In short all hell broke loose that wide afternoon.
By evening all was calm again. A crescent moon
hung in the sky like a parrot on its perch.
Departing guests smiled and called, "See you in church!"
For night, as usual, knew what it was doing,
providing sleep to offset the great ungluing
that tomorrow again would surely bring.
As I gazed at the quiet rubble, one thing
puzzled me: What had happened, and why?
One minute we were up to our necks in rebelliousness,
and the next, peace had subdued the ranks of hellishness.

So often it happens that the time we turn around in
soon becomes the shoal our pathetic skiff will run aground in.
And just as waves are anchored to the bottom of the sea
we must reach the shallows before God cuts us free.

To Be Affronted

For a while we caught the spirit of things
as they had drifted in the past. And we got
to know them really well. Cobwebs sailed
above the shore. Undaunted, the girl picked
them out of clouds, all being mysterious
and rubbery. Later a shroud lifted
them above the cement dream of taxis and life.
This was the more or less expected
way of things running out, and back
together again. What we couldn't see was
delightful. July passed very quickly.

More than the matter with it, more even
than circles coming undone near the middle
and the end, was the candle that stood in the vault,
muttering inclement things to the weather,
the gables. Imagine a movie that is the same
as someone's life, same length, same ratings.
Now imagine you are in it, playing the second lead,
a part actually more important than the principals'.
How do you judge when it's more than
half over? As pastel tundra
crowds in from all sides like a mandala
there is nowhere for the very little girl to go.
She plays with us, in our pageant; one is ashamed
at having been away this long and let whatever
get to the state it's in now. Too late, the boar's
head on the mantel glows in solitary
archetypal annoyance at the way time has just passed.

It's too late for the hussars and the bent figure
in the background: When I was young I
thought he was a wizard, or perhaps a forgotten
charlatan from a far-off capital. Now I'm not so sure.

Streakiness

Passing the low bridge, one's beads give vent
to a volley of abuse. The chestnut trees
shed their leaves one by one. Trying one
topic of conversation after another, the door
admitted visitors singly. Why not?

Was it for this we eschewed attention-getting
moments in the plaza after the sun
finished sulking? There were rabbits in the oasis
no one told us about, least of all
nougat merchants in close quarters. One
lullaby fits all. There is no clause in hearing,
only nimble perspective-gulping giants
or loneliness asserts itself, featureless
though picked out in pills of light.

Feverfew

It all happened long ago—
a murky, milky precipitate
of certain years then drawing to a close,
like a storm sewer upheaval. Road rage had burst its flanks;
all was uncertain on the Via Negativa
except the certainty of return, return
to the approximate.

Night and morning a horn sounded,
summoning the faithful to prayer, the unfaithful to pleasure.
In that unseemly alley I first exhaled
a jest to your comic, crumb-crusted lips:
What if we are all ignorant of all that has happened to us,
the song starting up at midnight,
the dream later, of lamb's lettuce and moss
near where Acheron used to flow?

But it's only me, now, I came because you cried and I had to.
Plaited bark muffles the knocker, but the doorbell
penetrates deep into the brain of one who lived here.
O brackish clouds and dangerous,
the moon is unambiguous.

Opposition to a Memorial

"Come back, in a few days."
—WILLIAM EMPSON

Not that it was needed that much, this much
was clear. A little cleverness would do
as well, a lei woven of servility
and something like affection. He would crawl through

the long days, dreaming of something else,
just to be near and not caught out.
A famished throng followed, always keeping
the same distance. What is it like to mend

and be shattered, weep and not know what you're
laughing about? The mother's tone was severe.
She spoke, but very little. It was time to go away
into the pageant night had promised:

There were prisms and lanterns at the outer edge
and toward the center a vacancy one knew.
This is what it means then,
to be in a dream and suck sleep from a jar

as though only the polished exterior mattered.
Inside all was crabbed notes and lines,
the reason of the doing. The reader frowns
and shuts the book. Another time, perhaps,

there will be effusions, random exclamations.
Today it's clear the rent has come due again.
And though you're offered a ride back, it's not so much
a favor as an occasion to brood.

What were the rights and the right ways?
Did we invest our strength in the kind grains
of conversation that blew across our page, and out?
Is this the time to tackle a major oeuvre,

or are we banished to shallows of content,
when one hears a companion curse and pick up the load
again, coming out into temporary sunshine and the past has waxed
benign, one more time? Is this launch definitive?

For Now

Much will be forgiven those
on whom nothing has dawned. But I wonder,
does our polemic have an axis? And if so,
who does the illuminating? It's not as though I haven't stayed,
stinking, in the dark. What does this
particular mess have to do with me, surely
one or more may have wondered. And if he
or she suddenly saw in retrospect
the victimhood of all those years, how pain
was as reversible as pleasure, would they stand
for nothing selling in shops now, the cornucopias
of bargain basements open to the weather?

From pantry and hayloft spiffy white legs
emerge. A way of sitting down
has been established, though it's the same stuff
we groped through before: reeds, old motor-boat
sections, skeins of herring. We brought something else—
some enlightenment we thought the months
might enjoy in their gradual progress through the years:
"sudden realizations," the meaning of dreams
and travel, and how hotel rooms
can become the meaningful space one has always lived in.
It's only a shred, really, a fragment of life
no one else seemed interested in. Not that it can be carried away:
It belongs to the décor, the dance, forever.

Image Problem

A strayed reveler or two, nothing unusual
for this time of year, zinnia season, yet one notices
the knocking in the walls at more frequent intervals.
One's present enemies stir in the evening wind
and atypically avoid the family room. After the big names
have grazed the steppe and moved on, a public silence
returns. Let it be the last chapter of volume one.

Some experts believe we return twice to what intrigued or
scared us, that to stay longer is to invite the egg
of deceit back to the nest. Still others aver
we are in it for what we get out of it, that it is wrong
not to play even when the stakes are spectacularly boring,
as they surely are today. The solution may therefore be
to narrow the zone of reaction to a pinprick
and ignore what went on before, even when we called it life,
knowing we could never count on it for comfort
or even a reference, the idea being to cut one's losses
on the brink of winning. Sure, their market research told
them otherwise, and we got factored into whatever
profit taking may be encumbering the horizon now,
as afternoon looms. We could ignore the warning signs,
but should we? Should we all? Perhaps we should.

Litanies

1.

Objects, too, are important.
Some of the time they are.
They can furrow their brow,
even offer forgiveness, of a sort.

You ask me what I'm doing here.
Do you expect me to actually read this?
If so, I've got a surprise for you—
I'm going to read it to everybody.

2.

Spring is the most important of the seasons.
It's here even when it's not here.
All the other seasons are an excuse for it.
Spring, idle spring,
you poor excuse for summer—
Did they tell you where they mislaid you,
on which arterial road piercing the city,
fast and faster like breath?

3.

It is important to be laid out
in a man-made shape. Others will try
to offer you something—on no account
accept it. Reflected in the window
of a pharmacy you know the distance you've come.

Let others taste you.
Sleep happily;
the wind is over there.
Come in. We were expecting you.

Like a Photograph

You might like to live in one of these smallish
houses that start to climb a hill, then fumble
back to the beginning as though nothing had happened.

You might enjoy a dinner of sandwiches
with the neighbor who makes concessions.
It will be all over in a minute, you said. We both
believed that, and the clock's ticking: Flame on, flame on.

A Kind of Chill

He had a brother in Schenectady
but that was long, long ago. These days, crows
punch a time clock on a forgotten tract of land
not far from the Adirondacks. They keep fit
and in the swim with lists of what to do tomorrow:
cawing, regretting the past absolutely.
That spruces up the whole occasion
and energizes them in ways they never dreamed of.
His afternoon was on a roll,
and, as with anything else, he got sick of it.
No claims to adjust. No hovering in dark alleys
waiting for a priest, or the police,
most likely, if this were the end of the fiscal year.

One Evening, a Train

Still at it, friend?
God likes us to find these things out
for ourselves. In many ways it's a crapshoot.
It's not that we're creeps, only a little strange,
like ice in ice cream. So guess what:
You're free to leave and take your shaving kit
with you. We've had our fill of your sort.

Majesté, excuse me. I was hoping for a little
cooperation here, a bending of wills, if you will.
You spoke to several people
and derived a law, one of less than six in this rough
hemisphere we call ours; it behooves us,
as we kneel, to look for black drops
in the hedge, all the while hoping for acquittal
of a crime we never committed, only witnessed.
It was as if growing up were somehow optional,
that one could choose between it and Chinese water torture.
We may not find the enemy, meet him,
invite him in, plant him in our caucus,
yet somewhere, fun will have happened
because of us. Now, about that résumé . . .

I liked one thing—wearing out the elastic
words along the wall. As the season grew serious
the garage seemed to stop breathing.
It was it or us, surely,
but how many more witnesses would come along
at that remote and, it must be owned, not
terribly auspicious moment? For it is seen
that when all the boarders have checked out,
one or two distinct crises remain to be finessed.
The welterweights, flyweights and bantamweights

must be administered to. In addition, there are highwaymen
to be foiled, or thrown somehow off the scent.
I'm afraid it's terribly complicated,
though simple enough when gazed at directly.

I don't know what her name is.
I don't know her well.

Mottled Tuesday

Something was about to go laughably wrong,
whether directly at home or here,
on this random shoal pleading with its eyes
till it too breaks loose, caught in a hail of references.
I'll add one more scoop
to the pile of retail.

Hey, you're doing it, like I didn't tell you
to, my sinking laundry boat, point of departure,
my white pomegranate, my swizzle stick.
We're leaving again of our own volition
for bogus patterned plains streaked by canals,
maybe. Amorous ghosts will pursue us
for a time, but sometimes they get, you know, confused and
forget to stop when we do, as they continue to populate this
fertile land with their own bizarre self-imaginings.
Here's hoping the referral goes tidily, O brother.
Chime authoritatively with the pop-ups and extras.
Keep your units pliable and folded,
the recourse a mere specter, like you have it coming to you,
awash with the new day and its abominable antithesis,
OK? Don't be able to make that distinction.

Old-Style Plentiful

I guess what I'm saying is
don't be more passive-aggressive
or purposely vague than you have to
to clinch the argument. Once that
happens you can forget the context
and try some new bathos, some severity
not seen in you till now. Did they
send for news of you? Were you forthcoming
in your replies? It's so long ago
now, yet some of it makes sense, like
why were we screwing around in the first place?
Cannily you looked on from the wings,
finger raised to lips, as the old actor
slogged through the lines he's reeled off
so many times, not even thinking
if they are tangential to the way we
slouch now. So many were so wrong
about practically everything, it scarcely seems
to matter, yet something does,
otherwise everything would be death.

Up in the clouds they were singing
O Promise Me to the birches, who replied in kind.
Rivers kind of poured over where
we had been sitting, and the breeze made as though
not to notice any unkindness, the light too
pretended nothing was wrong, or that
it was all going to be OK some day.
And yes, we were drunk on love.
That sure was some summer.

Well-Scrubbed Interior

Can you walk? I asked.
Sure I can, it said. I'll walk with you a little way.
We can talk about love and play
and the ocean that is always next door.

That's not quite right I said.
Sure the ocean keeps pace with us.
It would lose our respect if it didn't.
Mainly it just wants to be here and loyal.

That's what keeps it from splashing across the planet.
I can see you now it said.
I'm glad that you are in focus,
you in and out of dreams it said.

Often one will waken in a well-scrubbed interior
and find it looks dirty, or disappointing
in some other way. Just unplanned.

One keeps coming back to that.
There was little to be said, and we have already said it.
Here, I'll take you. You can repose in my arms
for the rest of the night, which will be blue
and gloriously understaffed.

Make that notoriously understaffed.

The bench is coming undone.

I recommend it highly.

Cliffhanger

In all plays, even *Hamlet*, the scenery
is the best part. Battlements, wintry thickets
forcing their edge on you, cough up their promise
as the verse goes starry. You will leave empty-handed,
others will know more than you. Time's aged *frisson*
gets to me more and more, like mice
in a pantomime. And then the prompter
throws up his hands in dismay. You *were* mortal,
so why didn't you say anything? Back to brick basics
for you, my man. We'll see another day
the wave coming up short at water's edge,
which in turn justifies our divagations:
We were *once*, right? Whichever saint calls out
of an awning is ours to succor and molest, else
why harp on the differences between us? Why castigate
what divides or loll on the boundary
that was almost always there?
                                        Infantas
would now intuit better fortunes if all
were copacetic between us, the corona lift its shape
into our ken, less warning than appraisal.
Now even the farthest windows have gone dark. And the dark
wants, needs us. Thank you for calling.

The Ecstasy

We wandered in and out of the lobby
of a large house in history.
There was little to see at first,
then our eyes growing accustomed to the darkness
we could make out figures on a bridge
who waved to us, seeming to want us to come nearer.

We decided not to do that.
You thought the place was scary.
I found it relaxing, invigorating even.
There was a smell of that kind of musk
that is less than a warning, more than a confirmation.
The furniture was all of a piece,
alas; the air moved nearer.
It was my breathing as I had often feigned it.

Going down the slope the next day
there was nothing in the brilliant, awful annals
that let us see
just to the margin, and no further.
I want out now.
I have traveled in this country
longer than anyone should, or has.
It's natural to want a little sweetness
along with one's hunger, to put nothing aside
for the blistery winter when friendships come unknotted
like tie-dyed scarves, and the weathervane's a mate,
only you can't see it pointing backwards.

We left early for the reception,
though swooning and sherbets no longer seemed viable,
and there was a hidden tax in all this.
Yet we stayed, longer and longer. The dancing came to an end,

then started up again, one had no say in the matter.
In the morning it was warm, period. I went out on some pretext
and stayed for twenty years.
When I returned you asked if I had forgotten anything,
and I answered no, only the milk. Which was the truth.

Filigrane

"I've had it up to here with water, and now
further spokes are coming undone.
Get me a copy editor, or a good stiff
drink, if you will. Our resources have been on hold
for a generation, and this is the result.
As usual, the region, a 'sensitive area,'
is being evacuated. No one knows how
long their toehold can hold out."

Our representative will be contacting you,
but meanwhile it is important not to move
or in any way betray your whereabouts to the listening
enemy. His sense of place is long,
but not endless. Mirage control has sealed the borders
with light and the endless diffidence light begets.
You may confess your sins to your mother
but not your aunts and uncles—one would fear
the cauterized result, and in this ugly, cliff-dwelling
universe risk bumping against the question again
in a minor key with too many sharps in it.
Please, would somebody try to telephone the delivery station
and unload the tears at the proper address?
It's *West* Fifth, not Southwest. A snowman
can point you toward the steps. Wheedle on
for just a little bit.

But I've been asked silly questions before. Now is not the
moment to turn on a dime, or even ask what saint
to pray to, given that they are all alike,
that is, holy. In the latest bewildering formulation.

Ukase

And as you were indulging in the thesaurus,
or, more precisely, being indulged,
the word-rabbits came hippity-hopping along.
Soon it was dusk. The weary river passed
to ask you the same song over again; the birds
(who knew it all by now) were silent;
and it was time to mold the analytical
to the time-sensitive. That is,
to say that it had happened and we were
no worse for it. Indeed, the sky
and nearby barns seemed about to chime
as we were getting our stuff together, ready
to leave, as always, though not quite decided
what tributes to accept, if night should bring any.

What a chump! Excuse me . . .
It is to the wind and the wildflowers I address these
afterthoughts, if they can be dignified
as such. And I digress, too,
in the gloaming where all can be finessed
as we are incurably, undeniably aging,
only I can't tell what that feels like—
It's so true! Not when, but if.
But we'll know it before it happens—we'll
recognize us from the way we look at each other,
not from any urgent movement forward
or anything like that.

Casuistry

The false dawn had been implicated, its circularity
seen as a rebuke to honest folks, a third largest city
of the brain. Others were quick to join
the fray. It wasn't our fault that so many
appeared specious in the waning light of February:
Who, indeed, would they appeal to?
There were no precedents for its apparent soundness,
not yesterday's dribs and drabs, the remnants
of someone else's feast, I'd wager. And what if
a lot of them come back and decide to settle down
with their parents, enraptured with home cooking
all of a sudden? Will they make the cut?
And what's out there for us on another
putative fine day? Oversubtlety? Our own quodlibets?

Andante Favori

In late summer we would call each other
over and over until the bitter foam subsided.
Was it a coincidence that letters began arriving
faster than fallen leaves, answers to ones
never sent, or so we thought?

In the end each piece fits neatly
next to another. Dust is wiped from the picture,
whose clear blue stings like a remembered promise.
Flocks are waving, dispelling tears that were premature.
The box has been left open—accidentally?—and light pours
into its subject, a late essay from the master's hand.
All around, brightness is forgiven, diverting
a lax sheen on letterheads and clothes
long hung in closets. We could try to leave
but the timing's wrong, borders are changing.

Honor to him who sits and consults
his illustration. The backward weave
of the waves congratulates him.
Pilgrims scatter slowly. Eccentrics die or live,
but each casts starshine on the pebbled surface,
commanded to sleep, stay or recuse
a melting pince-nez, spin out a foppish hour.

The Handshake, the Cough, the Kiss

For the clear voice suddenly singing, high up in the convent wall,
The scent of the elder bushes, the sporting prints in the hall,
The croquet matches in summer, the handshake, the cough, the kiss,
There is always a wicked secret, a private reason for this.

—W. H. AUDEN, "At Last the Secret Is Out"

When they passed through a city, it was others knew it first.
The man claimed no lift in his shoe but an advertisement for the dance
left over from the last street but one.
A spotty youth pointed toward the policeman.
Someone downstairs had called for a cab;
it had arrived, was blocking traffic. The driver
seemed lost, and there were already passengers inside.
Did I know where the Cinema Kriter was?
Oh yes, I said confidently, in French. We
climbed in next to the others, who were nice, disposed to receive us.

Every year at this time of day I get a feeling
of a pain, like thyme or dried figs.
Nobody needs to know what is ailing me,
which is sad, but telling them would be worse.
I say, would you mind if I light up in bars?
There's no place left to smoke. I wonder about taxis.
I used to smoke in them, because it was forbidden in the subway.
That was before I gave up smoking,
watching the flies or files drift upward, thick in gray noon.

And if a child came over to play
it would be asked its name, then given a dose of brandy
so as not to play any more. We risked it anyway,
out on the ice where it darkens
and seems to whisper
from down below. Watch out, it's the Snow Queen,

one said. She likes playing
as long as she's not involved. That seemed to make sense,
but what was I to do, with no trains till morning,
and a good sense of humor, several ward heelers concurred?

Next day the hills were parchment,
good to look at from far away, which is
where we usually are anyway. I dressed hurriedly,
consumed a hasty breakfast. Now it seemed there were pairs
of people thronging, telling me what to do. Father in his little house
took a bath. It was almost time for the news.
We took a walk toward the cathedral.
It missed us twice. I think. The pavement
of white chocolate curves around,
a zebra crossing.

Did the islands ever get in touch with you?
Turns out the bill was sent
to the wrong address. We have no credit rating
any more. We must try to live without it,
and the unsuitable caresses of oldsters
gone to the gym or the country. One
wall features billboards offering a trip to the seashore
in forty-five minutes. With that, we
can pick up and get lost. Far into the night an argument
stitches its way. How long can we go on comprehending?

A lot, unfortunately. So get a life. It's been real. I mean really real,
like you can't imagine it. The city was leaving anyway,
closing its ranks behind him. Soon no one
would remember the boy in dross who used to come
and stare through the skateboards at the abandoned furniture warehouses.
Nor was this a reproach, not to him for coming

with his charts and other paraphernalia, for no one,
not even his mother, could figure out what to ask him,
or what outlandish reply he would come up with,
even if he answered, as indeed he never did.
So they got on well during the first semester.

The city and its pepperpot domes that day
were a good time to be in. Out from
lattices a pleasant breeze was wafting,
and in that breeze, mingled tones
of melody like adjusted spices. Then it was all over.
He felt well, who never said so. I don't know,
it traveled under him, until he was going to be sick
in the pit of his stomach, where ailments dwell.
Nobody had to remind the boy
to hang up his shoes that day, he was already in them,
hobbling off to the cobbler's to buy some new laces
of the kind worn in the port city of his birth, but never
noticed until this hour, of the flying kite, and the spitball
hanging down, trying to unlatch the year.

They all knew him in that ancient, wondrous and miserable town
as the local amateur historian and vendor
of a kind of chili only the houris knew about.
Then, turning his face away, he'd try
to guess the answers to their riddles. If correct,
a kiss would reward him. If not, a retreat
to a sheet of paper or promise to better himself
in huge academic halls some kilometers away, but they
didn't tell him this. There was no formal inquiry
into his tousled penmanship, for all it led him
unto the doctorate of his dreams and
a cottage close to the bridge traffic where daily

the seams are let out at evening. It was a pretty
enough place if quiet. One has to endure
certain systems, then profit by them later,

and we reject these. Oh I am sure it was as serious then
to be struggling as it is now. We were children, which made it easier,
but harder as well because we didn't know anything. Now we have survived,
you might say. New factors have entered the equation, but the surround
is as messy as ever and still limitless. The one district that accepts these
excuses is strange to us. Hanging out with Baptists,
drinking temperance beverages, is another kind of
education, to which one grows accustomed during the autumn nights.
It comes as no surprise to learn that winter is on the way,
with headlands and diamond aigrettes. And the lightness.

Still hungry? Read on.
A group of wilted children poured the tar
from where it looked out on a film
of ashes to the horizontal bars. Or
it was arranged to look like some other unknown hour,
a circumstance of such girth as to bemuse purple assailants.
Then he left the drum on. From the radiator to the city center,
it led to indecent bragging and imbroglios.
Perhaps it's time to
change the frequency of what is seen
around us, leave the palace and go home.
A chariot waits beside the door.
The way in is blocked by the entrance, near it.

They called and said
I was supposed to be thinking
of a way to revise the program,
let in some light and air,

bring in some new people with new ideas.
I was speaking with Drusilla Link about it.
Turns out many of our shared concerns are identical.
But—and here she was emphatic—
None of us knows the extent of the other's capacity.

Because of what ails the story
his dreamaround became more dangerous.
We went there.

Think that all is not as we left it.
And not dying for everything,
Karsavina paused, shrugged, got on
with it, got back on the bus,
north until a few weeks ago.
A collective European rhythm pierced the veil with sighs.
Out of the dust rose a new Ritz de la Riviera.
Why must it explode?

I don't know—spring came and went so fast this year,
sex on the river—and one observes it.
By the way, only minors are allowed.
Finally I just went to him and said—look,
if that's all you can bring to the table, why are we here?
We've got lots to do—more than our share. You can hear cars
revving up in the next valley, but there's still not enough time.
Only doubt, and suspicion, subsist. Cut the week in half.
Stir the ice-cube tray. Bring a sketch pad, a child's illustration,
a small investment, then more material as someone oversees it,
a harmonic convergence viewed through a flawed window, on pain of death.
And better to be finding out this way than across rued reminiscence,
O songbird! You asked us to believe
in you but the way was short. Our quondam companions persist,

a small, muddy group, adhere to the rival shore, ravenous,
and expire.

Believe it, they feel the air.
The tunes here are overstuffed,
the lyrics threadbare. I don't get out—I see them. Good my lord,
grapes and other oranges could eat people
once the drill had been proscribed, if we let them. Instead,
gamboling on rocks is the new theme nobody is interested in.
Maybe one day, old sweet reason, "the art of making truth prevail," will
    stimulate
hybrid initiatives. Meanwhile we, we only, take a back place to whatever truth
is coming on like thunderheads, all along the horizon, an academy
where losers file past, and the present is unredeemed,
and all fruits are in season.

Yes, "Señor" Fluffy

And the clouds fretted and flew, as though
there was a reason for their acting distraught.
There may have been, of course, but at this distance,
better to act dumb and accept the inevitable
as a long-anticipated surprise. Then if what lands
on your plate stares angrily at you and the other guests
"can't wait" to hear your reaction, why, it's checkout time
at the gazebo and no one will forget you too heartily
as the next-to-last spectator always glimpsed on the premises,
feigning the concern for the victim that marks you as the killer,
for sure. As for being in touch with you guys
another time, we'll take it under advisement.

So this moment's tremors mingle with others
on the departure platform. Who knew it would be this silly,
and so dense? Nevertheless, we have a right to know,
to have our impulses regulated and calibrated in the
interests of farther and fainter reaction-shots. Sure,
you'll get your rights read to you and sooner
than you may have counted on. Let the monotonous
group of listeners pump you for details, we'll provide
backup and terminal ecstasy at the way stations.
It couldn't have been any other way. You knew that.

What's your name down there?
Despite misgivings, the story clicks to a halt,
as always. The credits surge. People rush to leave.
The shiny cars of another era are coming
to take us where we wish to be taken, lest we
outstay our welcome and sink in the embrace
of another mood.

The Inchcape Rock

Prop up the "meaning,"
take the trash out, the dog for a walk,
give the old balls a scratch, apologize for three things
by Friday—oh quiet noumenon
of my soul, this is it, right?
You lost the key and the answer is inside
somewhere, and where are you going to breathe?
The box is shut that knew you
and all your friends,
voices that could have spoken in your behalf . . .

Why, what did you want me to do with them?
Half a document is sufficient to this
weather, wild time, excrescence, more.
Rumors sift across a bald apologia.
The feet are here.

Lacrimae Rerun

Say that the withdrawing day is ponderable,
the nattering voices of schoolchildren an obeisance
among others, or an homage to texture.

We had our season together.
Operatic in the city, we shifted mightily
the stress to other fulcra as they became available.

We never knew what prompted us to smile
or to embrace. That was part of the city's dynamic,
deep under the pavements. We dreamed of philosophy sometimes
in restaurants, or beside a chattering brook.

All our resources are being trained
on this critical juncture in our fates' history.
It's no longer a novel or nursery rhyme,

a catch or glee, but a sermon grinding on continuously.
They come to the back door these days,
asking for a piece of meat, anything.

Which is why we tend to forget mentioning specific names in our thank-yous.
Congrats to math and the sciences, music and poetry
and all the rest, including any I've forgotten.
Their day will come soon. But for now it's the haunted sky

over impossible ridges and hollows
that I wish to impute. Was ever anything
crosshatched so ripe with despair?

A Perfect Hat

I forget what it is I would rather be doing.
Floral and verbal, I am in the thick
of what I would rather be doing, jumping off a cliff,
rousing subordinates. There are just so many things
one would rather be caught out doing, like measuring the tree,
the swift shadow of which menaces us and bluebirds.
Oh the mill sang of many things but its wheel
was always rolling whether you noticed it or not.
The wheel that is still today but much larger.

It cautioned us to leave but we slept
the exact duration of the idea that never leaves us now.

So, Yes

Kids probably don't know what they're saying,
and we, we're one shy of all the stepchildren
it took to get here. In odder moments we'd contemplate
the swathe of water leading to the horizon
and pretend it was the grass had come full circle,
even to this sidewalk of cream and ocher brick. Those
who trespass against us slipped into rephotographed woods,
verifiable, at least for the time being.

He who stumbles at the brink of some great discovery,
perplexed, will endorse for many years
the fox and its entourage, part of some map
of life, he thinks. Emerging
from the shadow of his later career, he slides
into the contiguous states of America, all cherry trees
and floral tributes. It was right to behave as we have done,
he asserts, sending the children on their way
to school, past the graveyard. Evening's loftiest seminars
can't dim the force of that apostasy. So, yes,
others had to precede us, meaning we're lost in a swamp with coevals
who like us because we like to do things with them.
The forced march makes perfect sense under such conditions.
Let's celebrate then, let there be some refreshing change
overtaking all we were meant to achieve and didn't.
On the practical side it looks as though their team lost
and ours failed to languish, absent a compelling reason to do so.

Of the "East" River's Charm

homage to Samuel Greenberg (1893–1917)

We read memorial happiness and cover
Our tables with the great blossoms.
                    —S. G., "Ballad on Joy"

The teachings, good, bad, or indifferent, were a warning. It wasn't
going to be easy.

Other things too nasty to mention
mottle the chiffon of a chanson
so it can outlast your laundry condition.
In heavy armor's care
the suitors advanced temporarily.
Was it a comment on today's
mistrustingness, some "moreover"?

These are clad in various fleeting robes
that the tenor knows, as he sees them.
Songs are sung by this counterfeit
contralto to words written down,
and in tomorrow's haste forgotten.

So much for our sham naturalism,
ego, my brother, faster of us two.

Of what? Let me then ask you,
as tide picks up tab, river that between us grew,
mere commentary on agile literary thoughts'
dustbin commonplaces. Yet here and there a jewel
gleamed, night's dark fantasy, over before it began.
Hail to something! Let bliss be unbuttoned
in corners of the rash act's explanation of it.

And dyed two, one new, none knew
an honest periphery as other than rind
of rhyme. The perfect attention snowed
in sleep and no one asked their opinion
of the remaining gents, off on a new tangent.
"I have an engagement."

Manna fell to the ground in streamers
and this was OK,
I heard someone say.

Hectored by possibility, beset,
one withdraws into a corner of the inner corral.
Is this what you wished upon me?
Weren't all my cares naked ones,
and I detached, stalking the streets
like some beast?

Weren't we "apprised," hence good for rest
as long as the mirror accepted our tentative
good nature, our composure?
Others than our children chew rubber bands, cursing
not meaning. In the meantime a nap
prepares a surprise,
travels to no end, but we thought we had one,
but it wasn't over—then—yet the possible bares its teeth
in a grin like a long line.

Just a little critical wondering,
and even architecture finally
gives its reluctant consent
to city's barren din.
The inky eye constrains us to a neighbor's

plot, and all swims iridescently,
as though there were no whither,
or backing out of agreement on a good day
in one's unusual situation.

La Bonne Chanson

It was all he could do, someone shouted.
They leaned over and he was gone,
the body dissolved in spring filaments.
When they came faster, it was disaster, you
wouldn't believe how many supplicants defected,

and him all ready to rewrite history
if a chance footnote offered itself.
He even tried to laminate my horse,
said it would go better. O I tell you,
the things we had, too many

in our time, too many pebbles on the shore.
We came back later but most of them were gone.
A few shot back the light of the strict stars
and that was all I had to say to you. He'd get mad,
they'd banish us. We'd swim in steep delirium.

Feast or Famine

You'll hear a different story
on this side. Anyway, it happens
this way. It must be, if
it must be, but only on the ground,
and then, only if he tells it
this way. It's quite simple, really:
Light in the kitchen goes askance.
It's a stored-up nimbus
from fairly recent times when they
took architecture seriously.

Now it's only about interiors,
how they run into each other
promiscuously, or are gone.
Another day packed
with no realism, shouting, a
little fawning for good measure.
Then it's off around the cape
again.

I said, in times of war
we make good warriors.
In peace we are as nothing:
good dads or bankers.
But see where the tide is rising
for the umpteenth time, and try
to put a saddle on that. Then
clap your hands. The whole scene
or reef has retreated. There's
nothing much but undergarments,
which are OK, but they lack
the vibrancy of clothes. Say,
send me some, will you?

Imperfect Sympathies

So why not, indeed, try something new?
Actually, I can think of a number of reasons.
Wait—suddenly I can't think of any!
The present is here, its birds and bees,
fons et origo of life, *folie de toucher*
that infects even the civilized classes—
none of these are a reason to "start with" life,
though some are undeniably a veiled warning
back from the precipice where love dwells
along with fetishism and nympholepsy.
No need for these not to cohabit as long as the horses
can stand it.
                   Downtown was mesmerized
another year. Just who are these strangers
who come on so strong?
                          Yet it is good to remember
one's humble origins, and reflect
on how we came to look this way.
What were we thinking all along? Who charted
this anxious *mappemonde*, barren of side roads
and identity crises?
                     There comes a time when the fleece
fills your mouth, but there was so much left to say.

The Black Prince

It might be a footfall in the forest
or an outdated dispatch from the Mouse King,
saying, come back to the frontier, all is forgiven.

And he was lost, gibbering on the coast of some
uncharted isle. His gestures and speech made perfect sense
when taken together. It was only when the wind blew them apart
that they didn't matter, mattered only to some.

Forwarded

It's coming on six o'clock
again.
The sun rehearses an elaborate
little speech, strictly
pro forma—no, wait—
it's saying *something*, like
Be glad it's over.
We waited for you.
I loved you,
and these were the consequences:
bright nights, lit sea,
buttered roofs, dandelion breath.
The dream of seeing it all.

Next year let's live in harm's way,
under the big top. Incongruous,
blue will find us, and the sun.

Like the growl of a friendly dog
it backs up, shivers itself
out of here . . .

"Never heard . . . anymore."

They Are Still Rather Lovely

Ovid, in the infomercial, starts to monitor *his* pain,
then gives up trying. A second later the image is lost
through a nearly opaque glass transom. It was an ankle,
sheathed in ribbons. Now apostrophe, the very stuff of narrative,
shivers and turns spasmodic. Yes, the girls were here,
it seems to say, but all have gone down to look at the bridge.
You were careful about choosing your companions, did what
was expected of you, rose early to greet the punching ball,
shook droplets off the toothbrush, and like so.
Does it ever occur to you in what millennia we are standing?
Yes, the good stuff was poised to return, but the screen crashed,
and there is no help in us, over and under the now receding water.
I'd like to buy a definite article, but it's not that easy.
The yes-men must have their say. Patter of the stranger causing us
to be noted, hunted down under the dome. Written memorials are fine,
better if placed beneath glass in a cold room.
                              Where did the smitten
firemen go? They sent us compliments and a basket heaped high
with jellies and preserves, a small bottle of cognac to be taken
in the night, preferably in the early hours of the morning.

I look and stand down from this mess my memoirs have created—
it was all about foxhunting, wasn't it, and getting there
ahead of one or two others, who glance sheepishly
now, falling back one or two paces? Sure, it was understood
you'd win, then accept second place, but I can't say any of this
intrigues me still. I'll look out for your mother.
She's probably on the way back from school, calling to you
in your grown sister's voice. Can we have habits and still
rattle on like this, smoothly, from one decade to the next?
It all depends on what your pappy found behind the briar bush,
with you in seventh heaven, the unlikeliest ward to be trapped in,
once over the stile. The vehicle of winter begins its slide,

slow avalanche toward the truest sentiments, encrusted in rime,
or left out in the open for everyone to enjoy, slave master
and commoner alike. It's not its fault we anticipated its arrival
by several decades and are disingenuous, bursting
to tell the circumstances of having settled, then scattered
to the four points of the compass, an uncivil rout
but a necessary one for ending here, this way, this day. The fat lady
is working up a full head of steam. The conductor is smiling,
the sylvan backdrop is unscrolling. Can we have our presents now?

Thrill of a Romance

It's different when you have hiccups.
Everything is—so many glad hands competing
for your attention, a scarf, a puff of soot,
or just a blast of silence from a radio.
What is it? That's for you to learn
to your dismay when, at the end of a long queue
in the cafeteria, tray in hand, they tell you the gate closed down
after the Second World War. Syracuse was declared capital
of a nation in malaise, but the directorate
had other, hidden goals. To proclaim logic
a casualty of truth was one.

Everyone's solitude (and resulting promiscuity)
perfumed the byways of villages we had thought civilized.
I saw you waiting for a streetcar and pressed forward.
Alas, you were only a child in armor. Now when ribald toasts
sail round a table too fair laid out, why the consequences
are only dust, disease and old age. Pleasant memories
are just that. So I channel whatever
into my contingency, a vein of mercury
that keeps breaking out, higher up, more on time
every time. Dirndls spotted with obsolete flowers,
worn in the city again, promote open discussion.

A Litmus Tale

The scribes sank in wonderment.
This was not the hierarchical file to which
access had been deeded. It was something
far more wonderful: an opaque pebble in the grass.

I am almost always looking
for themes to break down to further my research
into backward climes of noon alienation and majesty.
One, a little farther than here,
resonates today with unusual candor:
my own take on the disheveled
frankness we all inhabit
at one time or another. Backing away from tribal sunshine
so as to inhabit a no doubt intact compunction of one's own.

The Binomial Theorem

Tragic, in these times of culture, to be divided
by a shortfall that is already riven in two.
The abstemious think otherwise, keep to themselves
in hazy rituals whose ultimate purpose
gets blotted out by new trends in passionate landscapery.

Are we better for it? I ask you. Subway chiming,
ghost pilgrims flowing through revolving doors.
All change reassures the nattering classes.
They can have what they want as long as nobody
much takes an interest in it. The

dim flood restores us to our senses. What time is it?
Or was it? Would you say those figures are accurate?
Did a dream publish you as you turned in sleep
to that other accessory, who waited so long
that the life drained out of his circumstance?

Imagine that you can have this time any way it comes
easily, that a doctor wrote you a prescription
for savage joy and they say they can fill it
if you'll wait a moment. What springs to mind?
Do you turn and walk out of the drugstore, intent

on the bus that stops at the corner of 23rd Street
and after an eternity pulls up with a hiss
just as the red light is changing to green?
You are out of breath and silly from running.
Someone standing near the door is doing a survey

of transit users. There's time to compose a strict
etiquette unfolding from the fan club to the sea. Hark!
It's unattainable. All the way home we argued about whether
refunds would be made in cash or against future purchases.
It's the only way, you said. We'll end up wanting these anyway.

Hungry Again

Since I could not shout
I stood near the spout
the rainwater was running out of.
The rain, sentries,
taxed me with appearing.
Soon it was all old as clay.

Why wait for another day?
You know this one is happening
and will be the same after it has happened.
Nothing will come to take its place
and that will be fine, good.
Though not inhuman, we can play
at what it would be like to be God,
and God will not take us away.

Another time I was at your house.
It was suddenly dark inside.
A wind swept past the bark
of some trees. It was overdue,
they said. All storms are inept.
It was time to find the mind-crystal,
pore over what we still had,
the huge resource we owed.

Promenade

My mind occupied by something,
I notice shoals of dry leaves
rattled by the wind, upsurging
like a dog that's starting to lie down,
and a voice like that of my mother says,
"Then you'll just have to learn
to do without it. The leaves are shells."

Another time the voice brings me
back from not too far away.
I was imagining sisters, how a door holds sway
over one's long life, only coming at the end
to a "foolish consistency,"
by which time one has passed all
the reasonable objections,
is on one's own.
And how can I care if this broad chair
is made of monotony, or whether
queer night had a hand in any of it?
It's time to return to the chances
one wasn't offered, that stain us blue.

All the reckoning is wrong.
What the caliph's calipers redeemed
isn't meant for us, far out
at the edge of Saturn's rings,
the drop-off, whose scent echoes and soothes,
though it's any day, as it is
(jabbering of the streets and above),
though quiet will adhere
to the reverse side, make its prerogatives known
another day, same day.

The Recipe

*"What did you have to go and do that
for, you fathead? Don't you ever get
tired of being noble?"*
—The Palm Beach Story

I hope you're not listening (but you are,
somewhere).

Do you still need the handkerchief? No,
just a permanent address.

I figured the exclusionary forces were back
on a roll. The "water balloon" effect
detonated, more rainbow than rain.

You have the papers, etc. So . . .

Lie in that grass. It's what we came for.
Nothing could ever be that velvety again,
so close to the ground. My gaze fathoms whiskers.
It wasn't to be. We were on the wrong set
at the wrong time, even as the cameras rolled.

"You must be Mary." "No, I don't believe we've ever met."

The recipe vectored a long-ago collision by a pier
in and out of fins of sun,
now labeled and put away, with much else,
and too little of what was needed
that particular afternoon
close to the source of warmth and confusion.

Did I say it would be like this?
Don't blame me. On the other hand, if you want to,
and I could be chandler, greengrocer, fruiterer,
fishwife, all-around good guy, we can handle it,
air differences, table mutual misgivings and
give in just once to the sound that brought us here.
Why not? I'm game. Say no to nothing is my credo
and pocket veto. All joiners are smooth, low-bidders
and incurable romantics alike.

I'll post the banns, send out invitations, polish toenails,
describe moot situations to the skeptical. You rest the same.

A Small Table in the Street

Less and less sightly, Lord!
The cheap shots you sent us yesterday
are back today in force, mouthing with precision
whatever wisdom is printed on the wrapper's
verso. Let no one draw strength from that.

Our climate turns its face toward the heights
again. This would have been a powerful
soul adventure in the old calendar.
Now it's just random effusiveness:
firecrackers and maybe shots in adjacent streets.
Well, have the car sent round
while we stumble toward this strange thing: an anomaly.

Don't think the wind is doing you a favor
by refusing to die down. It's your shirt or its,
though both of you are free
to grovel when and if it seems appropriate
to do so. Only don't fall back on the old excuses, i.e.,
action as an excuse for inaction. We're not children anymore.
Why not give real life a chance?
                    I was here
and did nothing about it. Therefore I am condemned
to the punishment of the just: long, loose-skeined parades
along service routes. Is there a perfect tense for that?

It, or Something

No hope for last night.
They're as much like that as anything—when I thought
of going upstairs it didn't occur to me
to stop at the landing. Even less
to walk back down, walk around
near the stairs, and then—oh why not—
go out, into the next room
or even outside. What
would be the matter with that?
All of us go out at times
and just as surely, we're glad to get back
in, where we can resume doing something
we abandoned before, some task or something,
even something quite silly if that's
the way we want it.

Strange beauty queen,
she neither slept nor swam.
There was an opulent reservoir at her door.
Many passed it admiringly,
threw stones in it, swore
to return another day when the weather
was as beautiful as it is today.

It's not certain she ever noticed it.

One of His Nature Poems

Other solutions proposed themselves.
We could move west, devote ourselves to entropy.
We could embrace in embrasures. That, on the whole,
sounded most promising. Or we could forget we ever met.
It seemed pretty distinguished on reflection.

Dragging the Pacific for starfish, like we do,
one fluctuates as a shadow, like one's shadow.
Painted truths can't always be lively,
nor unvarnished arabesques straightforward and cool.
This purity I'd like us to contemplate living in
isn't flummoxed by brandy and cigars.
It waits in the room of lost steps.

Everything has a silver lining; it's a matter
of turning it over and scrubbing some sense into it.
By then the last few spectators will have given up
to straggle home through a rude wind, mud, and chaos,
by land, sea, or foam, literate for a day but other-directed.

And Other Stories

As though illustrated by Wilkie Collins, he swans
along low-ceilinged corridors lined with servants' bedrooms,
searching the one inauthentic expression: Is it a bathroom?
At night denizens circulate. A scratchy phonograph
record confides the sextet from *Lucia*: What was it
they were singing, that mattered so much?
Lucia had her mad scene, after all; she was happy about something,
unlike the rest of us. We go on clocking
what's there to be measured. There's not much
we can do about it.

When the supervisor asked me to step into his office I felt like a bride
in a Veronese fresco: So much still to be done,
arrangements unkempt, guests to be invited
at the last minute. Luckily few of them knew,
since none came, or was it my imagination? Were the halls
full of people? Was I crying, was my little daughter being sent away
to a boarding school in the North? Her peach-blow cheeks
and rose-colored satin bodice indicated secret grief,
which was now flooding the place. We had to get back inside.
The clock was on the verge of striking. And you know something,

it never did! Not while I was there, anyway.
There were shouts, always the same, unusable shouts
and an angry wind starting up in the hedges
but unable to articulate, like me and the other guests.
Again it was time to flee. A lake of brambles offered itself
like a protective cushion to the outsider, you and me. This had been foreseen,
but like a migration, took on another sense
as it unfolded, the sky Royal Worcester by now,
a narrative that will endure for many years,
even if no one reads it. Class dismissed, he said famously. School's out
forever. Saddle the theremins, love is on the loose.

The Gallant Needful

The hat hasn't worn too well. Nor, come to think
of it, have the pants. The shirt and cap are negligible.
As for the drawers . . .
                  So it went. Time was running
downhill while the clothes gave out. No one
wanted to wear them any more, which was
understandable, given that clothes are a going concern
to many. Mended with gay stuffs, they'll serve
another time, tied like shawls around
a stovepipe.
               Farewell nightmares, simulacra.
All the time a little is growing. As soup is to stew,
so the sea to bubbling chasms that prop up the "meaning."
Nice is nice enough. Just don't expect thanks.

America the Lovely

If it's loveliness you want, here, take some,
hissed the black fairy. Waiting for the string quartet,
on the corner, denatured I wondered what the heck.
I'll have some too. They call it architecture,
I was told. Anything to sift the discerning
from the mob-capped mob, their stiffened fright wigs
marching against the breeze improbably back
into colonial dreams and days. See that polecat?
He's yours, if you want it. Only be careful what you ask for,
she warned. Here in hither Tartarus we have names
for jerks like you. Flustered, I released the emergency brake,
turned to warn the approaching others.

This was the real thing:
The flash comes handily, signs of its musing scattered next day
like hoarfrost. The glittering, the of-two-minds
pause to share a winter pear and notes on decomposition
glued to the door of the fridge.
Was it for this we journeyed so far
by prairie schooner from reassuring Pennsylvania?
Believe the nights are bleak now,
though perhaps no more than our earliest attempts
at love poetry in a house across the street.
Pagans do combat with other pagans,
men with two hyphenated names block access
to the embarcadero.
Palinodes charm our hearing
as new strictures emerge in the ruckus, belike, betimes.

Then it too went away.

Anticipated Stranger,

the bruise will stop by later.
For now, pain pauses in its round,
notes the time of day, the patient's temperature,
leaves a memo for the surrogate: What the *hell*
did you think you were doing? I mean . . .
Oh well, less said the better, they all say.
I'll post this at the desk.

God will find the pattern and break it.

Phantoum

Why his business was for sale I can't exactly expose.
The bonds of cheap thinking repositioned us anyway,
plus you had to be a ghost to appreciate it.
Like you see so many of them.

The bonds of cheap thinking repositioned us anyway.
We found us enchanting, whirled by our partners
(like you see so many of them).
Along for the ride was a nursery of goats

who found us enchanting, whirled by our partners.
All that day and the next the light waxed dim.
Along for the ride was a nursery of goats,
running early, kids now, if only for the ease of it.

All that day and the next, the light waxed dim.
The albatross held and dissolved in mid-mist.
Running early, kids now, if only for the ease of it,
we tagged along on the sand, waving until it shed a last outline.

The albatross held and dissolved in mid-mist.
The auks were squawking, the emus shrieking.
We tagged along on the sand, waving until it shed a last outline.
The purple emu laid another egg.

The auks were squawking, the emus shrieking.
Grape and cherry were the flavors. Later they added mushroom.
The purple emu laid another egg.
After that we didn't fit in any more.

Grape and cherry were the flavors. Later they added mushroom.
We were grape children, trying to cope in a mushroom world.

After that we didn't fit in any more.
They studied ball playing, swinging the bat.

We were grape children, trying to cope in a mushroom world.
That didn't go down well. Or did it?
They studied ball playing, swinging the bat.
After lunch it was time to quit over some girl.

That didn't go down well. Or did it?
Daddy Warbucks was sad, but kept his reasons to himself.
After lunch it was time to quit over some girl.
He excused himself. Europe was calling.

Warbucks was sad, but kept his reasons to himself.
The others were off in a far corner of the room.
He excused himself—Europe was calling!
Besides, he had to work on the scenario.

The others were off in a far corner of the room.
The unspoken word beckoned. "Look, I came back.
Besides, I had to work on the scenario."
Easy enough to say, if you're a ghost

and the unspoken word beckons. Look, I came back.
It was all about you, from day one.
"Easy enough to say, if you're a ghost.
What possible use could they have for this old iron pot?"

It was all about you, from day one.
Only you mattered, on the desks and on the building's façade.
What possible use could we have for this old iron pot?
And the game changed, or fell away.

Only you mattered on the desks. On the building's façade,
in cafeterias and on playing fields the crowds shifted
and the game changed, or fell away.
It's OK, it's only a flesh wound. It's almost healed.

In cafeterias and on playing fields the crowds shifted.
Why his business was on sale I can't exactly expose
(it's OK, it's only a flesh wound, it's almost healed),
plus you had to be a ghost to appreciate it.

The Loneliness

"Bound and determined" one writes a letter
to the street, in demotic, hoping a friend
will find, keep it, and analyze it.
This much the future
is prepared to vouchsafe, with conditions:
You could design something at home.
Another's peace of mind isn't your concern
until the day it backfires,
and consequences wash over you, leaving you brackish,
untried.

OK, I'll try again:
peaceful, this time. Of course everyone likes light
lapping at the boathouse door, dredging
stones with sugar. It's as though a message
remained to be harvested, paperwork from me to you.

And we thought we were lost.
How many times haven't we given up in despair,
only to be reminded by time
of the firmness of its commitment
to our well-being, or lack thereof?

On Seeing an Old Copy of *Vogue* on a Chair

For all I know I was meant to be one of those marchers
into a microtonal near-future whose pile has worn away—
the others, whose drab histrionics provoke unease to this day,
so fair, so calm, a gift from cartoon characters I loved.
Alas, the happy ending and the tragic are alike doomed;
better to enter where the door is held open for you
with scarcely a soupçon of complaint, like salt in stew
or polite booing at a concert he took you to.

No longer shall the grasses weave quilts for our revenge
of lying down on, or a faint breeze stir milady's bangs.
What is attested is attested to. To flirt with other thangs,
peacockish, would scare the road away.

Frogs give notice when the swamp backs up, and butterflies
aren't obliged to stay longer than they do.
Look, they're already gone!
And somewhere, somebody's breakfast is on exhibit.

A November

The spoon went in
just right,
stirred the coffee,
was removed and lay
on the saucer, silent.

The lost library
books fantasized
about where they'd end up,
not
realizing they already had.

I don't understand anything
he says, my friend
who comes over.
When he says delighted
I am just
as sure
he means weighted down
with affliction
or affection.

He can't have been bothered
by next year's list of things,
places left unplanted.
The government went in.
That's why there isn't room.

Sleeper Wedding

The bells smoking beside me,
the salad of Nevada
everywhere ankle deep,
my thirst for everything overtakes me.
Why am I with this sandwich
in open country?

Why do the dogs make merry on the shore?
The Celebes celebs attend
to what is right
and gooey.

I even brushed 'em.

The blue jays wanted to build a think tank
three thousand feet in diameter,
thirty stories below the earth or above it.
The king told me I was a master
who needed to study, but
a master all the same.
My answer was who needs kings.

And on that note
maybe we could have it a little warmer in here.

Pavane pour Helen Twelvetrees

I.

Abrasive chores were a specialty.
Then, suicide at fifty.

Not a back street that didn't reflect
meanness, and somehow, candor.

To be clasped by the awkwardly handsome Phillips Holmes
in an open carriage in Havana:
"St. Patrick's Day, don't it make you feel great?"

There were fiery landladies to cope with
and the usual drunks. Otherwise,
time passes, assuring vulnerability.

I was saying, you never get over
some of these lumps, that's what they're for.
Otherwise, you can abide in discretion,
or just plain bawl.

The clients are coming back. Quick, the moustache cup.

II.

All around us tides, provocation
of abstracted sky and water.
Praise bellies the azaleas. Yeah, praise
them too while we're at it, everything
deserves a modicum of praise, except those
who don't get it. There's more, in a sequel
God will ultimately be writing.

He turns the pages of a vast
octavo volume, brings forefinger
to chin. H'm, that one might have turned out
differently, if I'd been paying attention.
Let's revamp the casting call
in the sky, see whose talent effloresces. That way
there'll be something to talk about next millennium.
The birds hear and drop to the grass.
Fireflies communicate spottily, but accurately.
The whole project is plain.
The rushes look good.
It was for this you spun your little web,
dear, and have somehow been rewarded. It is written

that only the unlikeliest take hold.
Tomorrow there will be fireworks, and then,
back to the chain of living and dying,
pleasing and ornery. The process shot whereby
scenery overcomes tedium, porch sitting.

Tonight we have tension and oneness,
arcane, arousing. Forgotten starlets
and minor nobility are apt to turn up in it.
And so he said not to go,
is standing stuttering there
fluffier than a dream in the park setting
where we were accustomed to dwell.

Are You Ticklish?

We're leaving again of our own volition
for bogus-patterned plains, shreds of maps recurring
like waves on a beach, each unimaginable
and likely to go on being so.

But sometimes they get, you know, confused,
and change their vows or the ground rules
that sustain all of us. It's cheery, then, to reflect on the past
and what it brought us. To take stone books down

from the shelf. It is good, in fact,
to let the present pass without commentary
for what it says about the future.
There was nothing carnal in the way omens became portents.

Fact: All my appetites are friendly. I just
don't want to live according to the next guy's trespass,
meanwhile getting a few beefs off my chest,
if that's OK. The wraparound flux we intuit

as time has other claims on our inventiveness.
A lot of retail figures in it. One's daily horoscope
comes in eggshell, eggplant, and, just for the heck of it,
black. 'Nuf said. The deal is off. The rest is silence.

Asides on the Theorbo

It's OK they said, it's all right not to know
where any of this is coming from. Trust your judgment.
It'll get better, dear, she said, otherwise call in
from the field. They'll send replacements.

And if he was all in, how would that jibe?
Why it'll be perfect. The pensioners will never know,
nor yet the boot camp riffraff. She'll show you to the loggia.

From here it all seems like a miracle,
clean sweep as far as the eye can see,
old panaceas rewired and good as new.
We'll spell you on the curve. It should be
OK, if not we'll send in a search party
to bring out the wounded and console survivors.

It was everything we had always wanted to know.
She congratulated us on what we thought we accomplished.

Autumn Tea Leaves

All across Europe a partial eclipse
is checking in: Unsudden surprise
and its sister, weary impatience,
mark the flow once the sluices
have been opened a little. Then it just goes,
an impromptu horizon clipped to it.
                                   Therefore,
I ask what is special about this helix, if
indeed anything is. Can you see it,
its difference, distinguish among halftones,
fugitive tints, measure the rising level
even as it suffocates us? Time was
it all seemed like a party, even work
before the workers were expelled for the day.
Dreams were positive heaven then, not just
framed pictures for the sleeper's instruction
and, yes, delight.
                    So if the mercury plummets
again, as it's supposed to tonight, what shred
of blanket will you deem sufficient for the occasion,
dread or ecstasy, or just wanting to be covered?

A low-grade fever installs itself.
These were dancers once, with faces
and senses of humor. Which of course wasn't
too much to ask, and so she came through smiling,
good-natured to the end. The cakes that were served—
is there a record of those? Or leaves collected
in the hollow of a stump, something one
would wish to have included in the reckoning
even if it was never going to be reckoned,
or small sail breasting the apparent tide,
on and out of the forever harbor, just this once?

Objection Sustained

Like a French king, I
know and do not know what it is I am.
Suffering aimlessly, pointlessly,
I think I'm on the spot right now.

Other margins will invite us
toward life, pull out the stops
on a day's notice. Invitingly
the crowd stops, shrugs toward us,
passes some judgment.

Anyway, it happens this way.
The can of ice slipped and cracked.
All my worldly belongings weren't
so worldly anymore. Sometimes
in a dream the tremendous peachiness
of everything assaults you like a wave
you look back at, knowing
you saw it, already invested in
some otherness.

All of last week's energy preceded
us into the maze. We could hear their
surprise up ahead but were determined
to unravel our own opinion
on key issues. Gradually I lost
access to these. I don't know who the others are.
He died later in other films.

So Long, Santa

You were good to us,
but we've got to think these things
out for ourselves, check in with you
later—why did I say that?
Not everything has to be
as big and as full as earth.

After he found a million dollars in a slot
the boy persisted, dying without uncovering a lot.
It's good to be painful
because it will come round again
and we won't be ready:
Barbara Allen's cruelty, the night wind
biting at scarves, pedestrians hurrying along.

And if I so longed for you as
to make the original millennial blush go away,
us back to our pets, things we had
to learn at school,
I'd be ashamed of my distance
from you, for being indispensable
as time and cures—
just getting the right thing right, for once.

After finishing everything up
I pay a formal call to the broker.
Sherry is drunk
and it will soon be time to think of the next set of circumstances.
Oh hell everything is that way,
this way, that way, twisted in the sun
of endurance—

the back way in then,
the assertion of formality without
a celebration next time.
That's all any of us gets,
why I am happy with you, alone, just us.

Singalong

You watch in street clothes. Why not
accept the easy way, the one
that's offered? The kind one?
Because it isn't easy or kind enough.
It has to be hard
to have brought us this far.

Any time soon
we'll manage to build barns,
paint, lock the padlocks, waive anything
dire. That way, we think, it will keep
for us and for a while. Other
than that we sleep, nod
like reeds at the edge of a pond.
Those places left unplanted will be cultivated
by another, by others. Looking back it
will seem good. The majestic verandah.
All the ships numbered.
The hedges grazed
like autumn, or a blight,
like fruit.